"USE A DVD AS:

(1) A PHOTO SUBJECT, AND

(2) A COLOR TEMPERATURE METER"

BOB REWICK

"USE A DVD AS:

(1) A PHOTO SUBJECT, AND

(2) A COLOR TEMPERATURE METER"

February 2019

CONTENTS

I. INRODUCTION AND BACKGROUND

The term **DVD**, as you probably know, stands for **Digital Versatile Disk,** a device usually used for storing movies and videos, but also for software, computer files, and other applications. **CDs** behave similarly, but usually retain less information than a DVD.

DVDs and CDs are well known examples of diffraction gratings, such as you may have observed from prisms and water droplets. Diffraction occurs because of periodic rows of lines and ridges, sometimes 4-5 thousand per mm, that are engraved on the disk's surface. When light impinges upon this engraved surface, it separates the light into colors we see in rainbows and DVDs: red, orange, yellow, green, blue, indigo, and violet lines (**Reference # 1**).

A grating is sometimes called the substrate that supports the engraved surface, such as the film attached to a DVD's top surface. Basically, any regularly spaced arrangement of identical, parallel, or elongated configurations, such as overlapping screens of different mesh sizes, can act as a diffraction grating.

Many references describe diffraction properties for DVDs and CDs (**Reference # 1),** specifically for the absence or presence of desirable wavelengths from different lighting sources, such as sunlight, LED, tungsten and fluorescent, etc. But, the geometric arrangement of the diffraction patterns is seldom, if ever, mentioned.

Every lighting source has a different wavelength composition, i.e. color temperatures and white balance (WB), which change with atmospheric conditions, the time of day, and even with the age of the bulb. For example, WBs can radically change for sunlight over the course of a day, from 5,000-6,000 K at noon, to over 10,000 K late in the day (K = degrees Kelvin).

A variety of WB settings are found on many cameras, which should be adjusted to match the WB of the actual lighting source; if a different WB is selected on the camera, a photo taken under these conditions will usually be bluer for fluorescent and redder for tungsten. In many cases, however, the automatic white balance (AWB) setting provides good results.

If more accurate WB results are needed, especially in mixed light situations, you may; (1) want to rely, or program around, a color temperature meter's readings, or (2) use custom white balancing (**Reference 2**).

But, rarely, if ever, will you find much literature about: (1) the reflection potential of a DVD to create exciting photographs, (2) the observation of different DVD lighting patterns, and (3) how these pattern differences can be used to identify lighting sources, without using a color temperature meter.

The objective of my **Book** is to answer some of these concerns and questions.

II. DVD LIGHTING

In my studies, I examined three types of lighting: LED (light emitting diode), tungsten, and CFLB (compact fluorescent light bulb). I chose LED over sunlight because the latter has such a strong time-of-day temperature dependence

III. PHOTOGRAPHY

My studies involve photographing DVD-R disks on which I place on the disk's colored areas, reflective subjects, soap solutions, and soap bubbles,

I used a Panasonic TZ5 point-and-shoot camera, yes, a very old model, but still capable of taking excellent photos. I didn't use a DSLR or tripod because of space restrictions; thus, all the photos I show are hand-held. For some photos, I used a Nikon P900, in its macro mode.

To reduce camera shake/blurry image problems, I generally take 3 burst shots, a 2 sec. shutter delay, an ISO value of 400, and an auto WB (white balance) setting.

The angle at which a DVD is illuminated is critical. No colors or patterns are usually observed at a 90-degree angle of view, often only the reflection of the lighting source; an approximate 45-degree angle of view usually provides the first appearance of the colored patterns.

IV. RESULTS

A. PATTERNS

When I examined the above 3 lighting sources, I was surprised to discover that a disk's diffraction patterns depended on the light's origin, which was not mentioned in the literature I reviewed.

Below, **(IV A, photos 1-3)**, I show you photographs for the 3 diffraction patterns I observed for LED, tungsten, and fluorescent lighting.   You can clearly see the dependence of the observed patterns on each lighting source.

LED LIGHTING--PHOTO #1

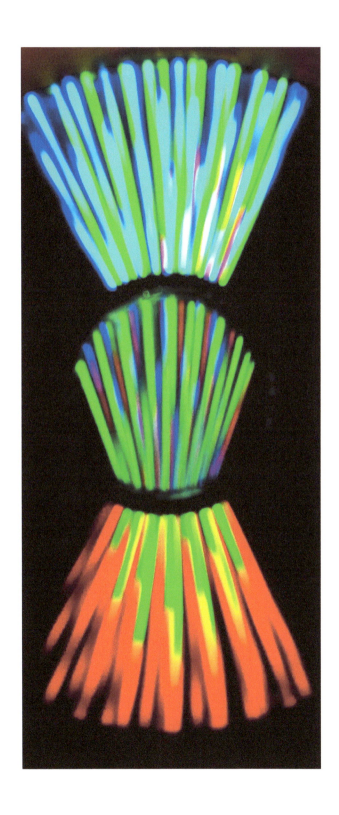

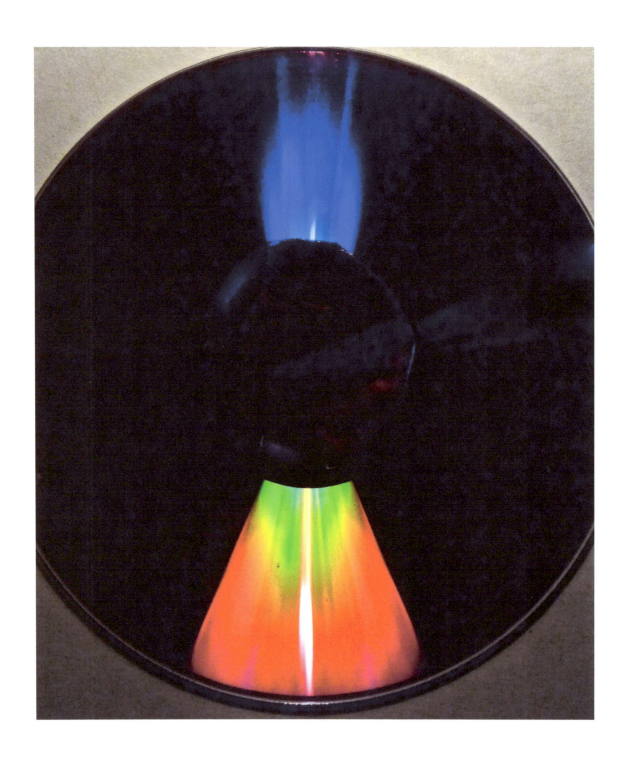

FLUORESCENT LIGHTING--PHOTO #3

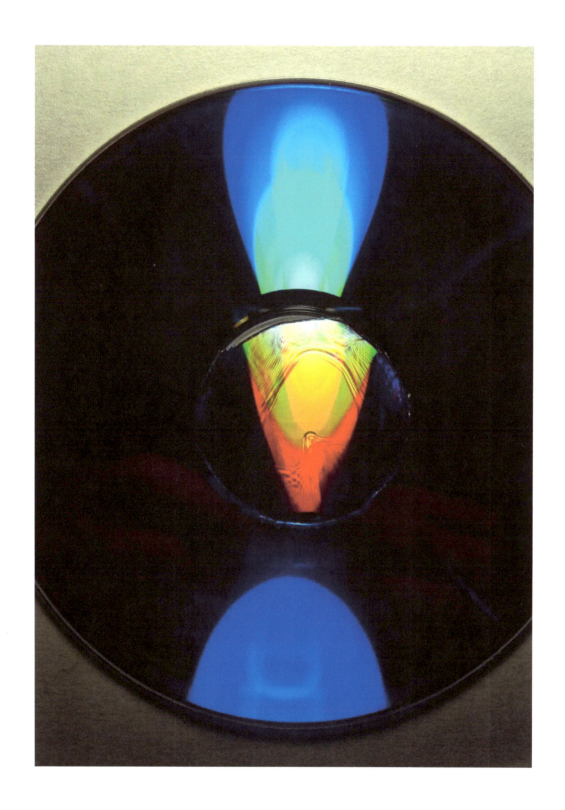

B. REFLECTIONS

As you most certainly have observed, DVDs have strongly-reflecting, mirror-like properties, which when combined with diffraction patterns from a DVD disk, can create some unusual images, which I show you in the following photographs, **IV B, photos 1-5.**

REFLECTION--PHOTO #1

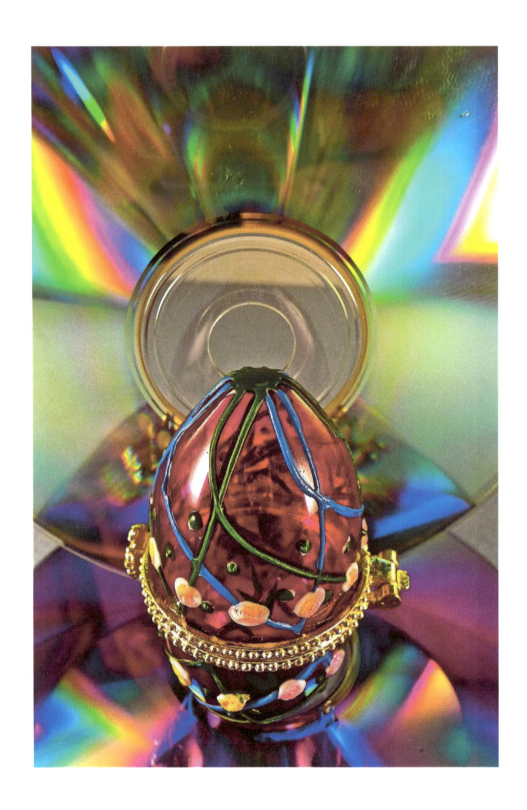

REFLECTION--PHOTO #5

C. Soap Bubbles

A conglomerate of soap bubbles can easily be prepared by shaking, stirring, or agitating many commercial soap cleaning products, such as those used for dish washing and shampoos, etc. Then, by using a spoon, I transferred some of these bubble layers to the top of the diffracted DVD color patterns.

Below, **IV C, photos 1-3,** I show you photographs of these soap bubbles on a DVD disk, on which you can observe three important optical properties of DVDs: diffraction, reflection, and interference. For discussions on interference, please see **References 3-4.**

SOAP BUBBLES--PHOTO #1

SOAP BUBBLES--PHOTO #2

D. Soap Solutions

In the following two photographs, **IV D, photos 1-2**, I have placed several drops of a commercial dish washing soap solution onto the disk's colored line patterns, which slowly spread over the DVD's surface, in formations resembling the disk's line engravings.

SOAP SOLUTION--PHOTO # 1

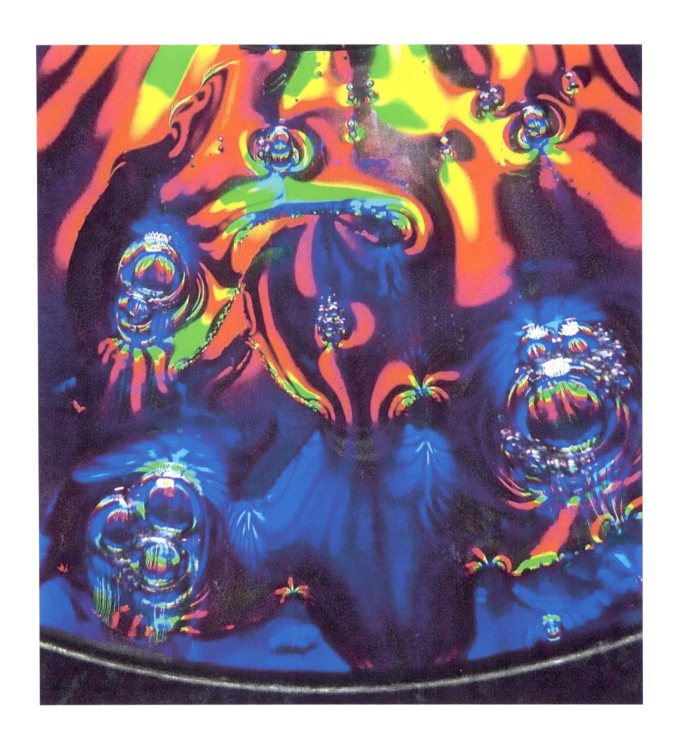

V. SUMMARY AND CONCLUSIONS

No doubt we all see colors in DVDs and CDs when they are positioned correctly in sunlight, and thus should be considered diffraction gratings, such as prisms. But how many of us, including photographers and most of my reference sources, report that a disk's diffraction patterns differ in complexity and lighting colorations depending on its illumination source? Probably very few.

I was surprised to make this observation during my studies using DVDs as photography subjects, and surmised that perhaps the observed color and pattern variations might help to identify what lighting source was illuminating the disk.

I discovered two other literature sources (see **Reference 5-6**) which hinted at the same concept, but only considered daylight and fluorescent lighting, with no supporting photographic evidence.

For example, this literature only cites the presence or absence of a green diffraction line to verify that the lighting is fluorescent.

But, in my studies, where I evaluated LED, tungsten, fluorescent and daylight illumination, I found the green line fluorescent determinator to be tenuous at best, and that the overall diffraction pattern was a much superior indicator of which lighting was present than a single line.

Moreover, the latter two references only vaguely refer to how to use DVD diffraction patterns to identify lighting from many sources. In my research, I have studied several other sources in addition to photographing the intense and abstract color patterns I view on a DVD itself, and especially in the presence of other reflective objects and liquids.

I show photographs of all my results earlier in this text.

But most of all, I am very excited to show that a simple DVD can distinguish lighting from difficult to approach positions, such as bulbs on high ceilings, and even throughout the day when color temperatures can change significantly.

I realize that WB mis-adjustments can often be easily corrected by a computer, or even by applying the auto WB Control (AWB) knob on my camera, but the disk method appeals to my basic desire for simplicity in all of my camera operations.

I conclude from my studies that: (1) the effects I observe are repeatable, (2) a $0.25 DVD can duplicate some readings that the $1,200 **Sekonic Model Prodiji C-500** color temperature meter can generate, but at a cost of only about 0.02 % that of the meter, and (3) mixed lighting conditions will probably be difficult to resolve.

On your next photo outing you can conveniently carry a DVD in your coat pocket or camera bag. For quick reference, you might also want to include photographs of DVD diffraction patterns I have observed, or images you have created yourself, attached to 3" x 5" note cards.

Finally, when you come across a **"once-in-a-lifetime"** scene you don't want to miss, and need to record the most accurate WB setting possible, use a DVD to make a rapid qualitative WB estimation.

VI. REFERENCES

1. **"A DVD As A Diffraction Grating"**, Google on the **Internet.**

2. **"How To Achieve Color Accuracy In Your Photographs By Using Custom White Balancing",** Bob Rewick, www.Amazon.kindle.com.

3. **"Soap-Scapes—How To Photograph Soap Film Color Interference Patterns",** Bob Rewick, www.Amazon.kindle.com.

4. **"Soap Bubble Photography",** Bob Rewick, www.Amazon.kindle.com.

5. **www.cinematology.com.**

6. **www. photo.stackexchange.com/questions.**

VII. ABOUT THE AUTHOR

I am a professional photographer and a research physical-inorganic chemist. I worked at Gulf Atomic Labs for 3 years, SRI International, Menlo Park, CA, for 32 years, and 3D Technology Labs for 8 years, where for some of these venues my chemistry research was considered of international importance.

In about 1985, I began taking many classes, workshops, and seminars from well-known photographers, such, as Galen Rowell, John Shaw, George Lepp, Bryan Peterson, and others, and at Foothill and San Mateo Colleges.

I have been a member of 4 camera clubs in the Bay Area, currently with "Friday Foto Fanatics" (FFF) in Campbell, CA, where I lecture, display my work, and serve as an advisor.

I have exhibited my work at several San Francisco Bay Area venues, including Stanford University, Palo Alto, CA, SRI International, Menlo Park, CA, and the Coyote Point Museum, San Mateo, CA, and others.

In addition, I have received certification from: (1) the Nikon School of Photography, (2) the Canon Masters School of Photography, and (3) a seminar on how to judge camera club competitions.

I have travelled extensively around world, and serve as a photography judge, a teacher and a lecturer on a wide variety of photography subjects for beginning to advanced students.

I am co-owner, with my wife Joy as my editor and viewing scout, of **"Photo Expressions"**, a business concerned with teaching the **"art"** of photography, and learning how to **"see".**

I have a preliminary website (Google the names "**Joy and Bob Rewick"**), where some of my very early work can be seen. A more current website is under development.

I have published 33 photography books/articles that cover basic to advanced techniques, some of which have never been reported, or are advanced editions over what has been only briefly mentioned by others.

VIII. CONTACT THE AUTHOR

For comments, suggestions, criticisms, literature references I have missed, and even praise for my **Book**, or just to discuss photography in general, please contact me at bobrewick@gmail.com., or 650-254-0110.

www.ingramcontent.com/pod-product-compliance
Lightning Source LLC
Chambersburg PA
CBHW041433050326
40690CB00002B/535